GOSPEL REFLECTIONS

FOR SUNDAYS OF YEAR C: LUKE

First Published by Messenger Publications 2015

ISBN 978-1-910248-22-5

Designed by Messenger Publications Design Department
Printed in Ireland by Naas Printing Ltd

MESSENGER
PUBLICATIONS
JESUITS in IRELAND

Messenger Publications,
37 Lower Leeson Street, Dublin 2
www.messenger.ie

GOSPEL
REFLECTIONS
FOR SUNDAYS OF YEAR C: LUKE

DONAL NEARY SJ

ACKNOWLEDGEMENTS

The author is grateful to Logos Press in whose missalette these reflections were originally published. Further reflections may be found each week in the current Logos Missalette. He also acknowledges his dependence on the commentaries on each gospel and the Acts by Fr Michael Mullins, of Waterford Diocese (published by Columba Press).

Currently Fr Donal Neary is editor of *The Sacred Heart Messenger* (www.messenger.ie), and National Director of the Apostleship of Prayer. Native of Dublin, he lives in the Jesuit community at 35 Lr Leeson St, Dublin 2, and is also involved in retreat and pastoral ministry in Ireland. Previously he was the chaplain in Mater Dei Institute of Education, Parish Priest in Gardiner Street and Director of Tabor House, Milltown Park. He has also done summer work in India (Calcutta, Assam and Darjeeling), Tanzania, and Zambia.

Fr Neary is author of *Forty Masses with Young People* (Columba Press) and *Who Do You Say That I Am* (Veritas). He has recently contributed to *Handbook of Prayer in the Catholic Tradition: Learning, Practicing, and Sharing Spiritual Intimacy* (Ed. Robert Wicks, Ave Maria Press).

Further books in this series are planned for each liturgical year.

Royalties from this book will be given to the Jesuit Educational Apostolate in Assam, NE India.

CONTENTS

INTRODUCTION

A connecting thread through many of the reflections in this little book is the link between faith and life. A constant theme of St Ignatius of Loyola is that of 'finding God in all things'. A reflection for each Sunday gospel in Year C makes links of life and faith, faith and personal stages of development, and the gospel reading.

Their source was a Sunday homily, mostly in St Francis Xavier's Church, Gardiner St.

In his encouragement about the homily, Pope Francis writes: 'The homily can actually be an intense and happy experience of the Spirit, a consoling encounter with God's word, a constant source of renewal and growth.' These reflections aim to be something like what he recommends – *The Joy of the Gospel*.

The preacher must know the heart of his community in order to realise where its desire for God is alive and ardent, as well as where that dialogue, once loving, has been thwarted and is now barren.

What the book is *not* is an exegesis or scriptural commentary on the gospel, or a link between all the readings. Many books highlight these areas. These reflections can also help towards preparation of a theme for Sundays in a liturgy group, or to prepare to hear the gospel reading or to reflect on it during the week. They also might help with composing the Sunday homily.

Above all, may they bring us closer to the Lord Jesus who wants to come close to us in his word, and his word is a human, loving word.

Donal Neary SJ

1ST SUNDAY OF ADVENT

Slow waiting

The four weeks of Advent are a slow wait: one candle this week, the empty crib. With Mary and Joseph we wait for Christ. The candles light the way for them – and for us, one each week of Advent.

Christmas should come quickly – the message of the ads. We could be excused for thinking it is nearly over. The Christmas parties are well under way. Some dinners for the elderly have been held already. The carols have been playing for weeks now.

The best waiting, like waiting for birth, is slow. Parents wonder about their child – who will he/she be like? The mother needs support and love; the children look forward to another baby; grandparents wait in pride. Even when the family situation is limited, we wait in joy and hope for the child – like Mary and Joseph, Elizabeth and Zechariah and all the bible parents who waited, often for many years.

How is my faith this year from last year? And what would I be asking for? Would I promise anything to help me wait actively for Jesus – Mass more often than Sunday, the Angelus every day, to read the gospel each day, to be kinder and more just, care for the poor and needy at home or away. Let my Advent bring me closer to God and effect for the best the lives of those close to me. If we wait in faith and in hope, then everything, even the carols sung too early and the celebrations too early, can remind us of the God who is coming soon in Jesus Christ, to be born of Mary.

Mary, may I wait with you in joy and in patience and in hope.

2ND SUNDAY IN ADVENT

All reminds us God is near

A poet wrote: 'when I am an old woman I shall wear purple', to remind her that life can be different day by day, or that she might be personally noticed and change her life.

This time of the year the Church wears purple and we remind ourselves that Jesus is near, that life can be different and that we can change our lives.

The gospel from John the Baptist encourages a change in our lives. We would look on ourselves and regret what we should regret – our sins, our meanness, our minor faults and failings, our injustices and hurt of others. In his time the people would immerse themselves in the river and be forgiven. We can immerse ourselves in the healing and forgiving love of God in many ways, including the sacrament of reconciliation (penance, confession). We can immerse ourselves in the mood of waiting for Christmas, and take this on the spiritual level and well as the ordinary.

All of the weeks of Advent can be a preparation for the way of the Lord, which we will hear of during the readings of the coming year. This is a time of joyful waiting, knowing we cannot be let down. The purple of Advent is not the purple of mourning but of joyful anticipation – like when we dress in the football team's colours early in the morning to look forward to a match.

If we take time for the spiritual preparation with some prayer, sacraments (maybe go to Mass once or twice a week, or daily for Advent), and if we help our neighbour a bit more than usual, then nothing of all the preparations can be just secular. Everything of this month can remind us of God... trees, lights, carols, parties, Santa hats, cards, gift-buying – big reminders that God is near.

Give us this day our daily bread and daily truth, Lord God.

3RD SUNDAY IN ADVENT

Brings Out Our Best

This mid-point of Advent alerts us to issues of justice and equality. The prophet John has been asked as a sort of trick by people who exploited others with tax bills, and soldiers who often used their brute force on others, how they should repent. His words were tough but quite ordinary – don't overcharge, share your surplus with the needy and don't exploit people. It's another, but more figurative way, of stating the basic demands of 'Love one another'.

Christmas can bring out the best in us to care for the needy. We are surrounded by charities looking for aid. We know that Jesus hears the cries of the poor, and he joins every carol singing group trying to help.

Christmas also asks us to consider our honesty and integrity, for we know that many are poor, at home and abroad, because of the greed of others. Christmas is a reminder and a challenge that all can live with the dignity we have come to regard as human rights – education, safety, shelter, food, water, employment, freedom. The Christ child who was born poor represents all the poor of the world, especially children. As he was born ordinary, he represents that God meets, greets and helps us in the ordinary aspects of life.

The one who is to come is the one who will live and love according to these truths of human dignity and equality.

Come, Lord Jesus, child of the earth, child of God.
Come into our world of joy and sorrow. Stay with us always,
now and at the hour of our death. Amen.

4TH SUNDAY IN ADVENT

Sharing and celebrating faith

One of Mary's first recorded journeys was after the announcement to her that she was to be the mother of God. It was a journey of service, a visit to her cousin who needed help. When dealing with such challenges as pregnancy, bereavement, redundancy, a son in prison or a daughter on drugs – we want to talk and we want support.

Mary and Elizabeth had something else to share – their faith. The prayers they said have been said ever since. The stage was small but the audience has been millions ever since. They were not shy about their faith in their God.

In a time like ours we need to externalise our faith – to go to Church, send a card with a Christmas greeting, not just a season's wish – not to parade, but to make present our faith.

The meaning this week is – *Jesus is born, and we celebrate that together*, with thanks, music, socialising, prayer and Mass. We need to find God again, and let ourselves be open to him in the deepest areas of life, just like the husbands of both these women, Joseph and Zechariah, as well as their wives, were open to God.

Nothing need keep us from God or from the crib at Christmas. All are welcome. The real meaning of Christmas is to meet with God and to help our neighbour.

Come Lord Jesus and bring joy and laughter among us. Come with the music of eternity and the songs of the earth. Come among us and make us truly grateful for your birth and your love.

CHRISTMAS DAY

God made flesh

In a country church there was a whitewashed wall – maybe you heard this story, but like the Christmas story it's a good one. As people came in, they bowed to the wall or blessed themselves passing it. People wondered why, as there was no picture on the wall. At a time of repainting the church, the whitewash and a few layers of paint were removed and a fresco of the nativity was found. The ritual had remained when the reason was forgotten.

There are many customs and visuals of Christmas, houses are lit up with stars, reindeer, and baubles – everything to celebrate that the divine mixed with the human in an intense way, the family of heaven and earth joined, when light and hope shone on the world. Some reminders are more direct than others. Others may be a bit like the fresco – still there and yet we wonder why. Let's stop saying put Christ back into Christmas, say rather find Christ in all of Christmas.

In every face you see this day, think of the face of God. We often pray that the face of God may shine on us, when we are brought face to face with God we will be face to face with immense and enduring love. We long for this now and forever.

People long for justice, for peace. People long for just enough in life like street children of Calcutta and children all over the world, and we long for reconciliation. Christmas is also a reminder of them. Not alone of God's immense love for all, but for the immense and enduring torture as God suffers still today in us all. The cross is in the crib, reminding us of the future of this child.

Also – enjoy all the reminders of Christmas. Let everything secular about Christmas remind us of its holy meaning. Every light you see, every red nosed reindeer, every cracker and bit of pudding, every bit of love under a mistletoe, in them all see, and be aware of Christ in everything of these next few days; and be glad of the face of Christ made human for us this night.

FEAST OF THE HOLY FAMILY

Various aspects of family life are highlighted in the readings today. They are chosen with family life in mind – the old, the young and the child – and in praise of family life with both Elkanah and Hannah, and then Mary and Joseph coming close to God in their family life. Today is a day in praise of family, marriage, sexuality, birth and of prayer for families. And in the family we learn about God – more by example than by words.

Most families manage well even in times of stress. Daily and ordinary love can overcome a lot else.

While praising the great efforts of parents today, and the strong family life which exists among us, we also look at contemporary problems: the stresses on the one-parent family; children unsure of the commitment of the parents; the effects of divorce on the children, and admitting that marriage breakup has a confusing or damaging effect on children; the long life of elderly who are very ill and require a lot of loving but difficult attention; the effects of addiction to drugs and alcohol; prison and crime.

Faith, prayer, Mass and the Church can bring us through a lot in bad days.

Prayer can be a valued part of family life. In all the different stresses today of family life, if we teach by word and example the value and place of prayer in their lives we have given a lot. The example of love and care, even in stressful times, can never be underestimated.

Some prayer at night or in the morning, before a meal or leaving the house; Mass, and including prayer at high points of family life are ways of including prayer in family life. Family is the school of faith and the place of God in the ordinary everyday world.

Jesus, Mary and Joseph, help us in our family life.

2ND SUNDAY AFTER CHRISTMAS

Christmas: family feast

Jesus grew up like all of us in a family – coming from the family of heaven to that of Mary and Joseph and their extended family. We know his grandparents' names; he had cousins and he didn't get on with them all; he had an aunt as the wife of Clopas.

All of us are children, some are parents, some are grandparents, aunts and uncles. All play an important role in the lives of the family – the younger generation. Where Church and state strengthen and support parents and children they are doing something essential.

None of us has the perfect family. Families include people with all sorts of difficulties – alcohol or drugs, crime and prison, people who don't talk to each other; families who had to leave home and come to Ireland for work, or leave Ireland for work. Joseph and Mary had their family difficulties – their child could have been killed by a mad king Herod, and they couldn't go home for fear of him; Joseph died leaving Mary a widow, and Jesus was murdered in front of his mother. The holy family know what family life is about, and our faith is a support to family life.

In our family we learn most of the important things of life. We salute today families who survive and support each other in difficult times: parents bringing up their children in a one-parent family; grandparents making sacrifices for another generation; people widowed and living now without their loved ones; adoptive and foster parents. We thank our parents and families for sacrifices made to bring us up.

Jesus, guide us in life;
Mary, look after us;
Joseph, pray for us.

BAPTISM OF OUR LORD

Spirit energy

Today, Jesus' baptism by John, was a special moment – the real coming of God's spirit upon him. It was the same Spirit who had come upon Mary at the moment of Jesus' conception, and would come to Jesus at his last moment on the Cross.

The spirit brings him new energy. The feast marks that something new is happening, and that Jesus is the beloved and son; from eternity and into time.

The Spirit came upon him – but not just for himself. He would send the Spirit later to us – of forgiveness and of perseverance in doing good.

Today is about energy. Jesus found a new spirit in himself after his prayer and he heard words he would never forget. Maybe you have heard words of love from someone you will never forget. They give energy to the heart and soul, making us people always on the go, ready for new life within us.

The Spirit pours the energy of God into bread and wine and they are changed forever. He sends himself forever. It is sending the love and presence and energy of God.

We know that we can get stuck. We need new infusions of the Spirit to give new energy. Can we be the type of people who others think it's good to meet? Open to the spirit of God, open to new life, new love, being really fully the person I can be?

May the waters of baptism, O Lord,
bring us the new life of your love.

1ST SUNDAY OF LENT

Jesus tempted off course

Jesus was brought out of the ordinary into a place where he was tempted off course with three temptations – to comfort, power, and wealth – three things that can take us over. Money, power and comfort can lead us astray – when we want wealth, to be no.1 and prioritise comfort in various ways. The words of Jesus are to use all in service of God and the neighbour.

He goes back to the word of God to find strength and insight to fight off evil – to the words he learned at home, and at school.

A big source of energy for us is the word of God. On Ash Wednesday the invitation was to believe the good news. That is where we may find life and strength.

We remain in the Church because of Jesus Christ. The word of God in his gospel remains life-giving and strong. Today's scripture shows us that temptations happen often to take us off the path. So too does the unexpected, and scandals have happened in many of the national institutions. Church life may leave us down and weak, but the spirit who kept Jesus strong in the desert will do the same for us.

A Lenten thing to do could be to read a bit of the gospel every day. Look up Sacred Space on the web and pray from that. Or Pray-as-you-go. Pray your own favourite gospels. Read the gospel to the children. Hear the word at weekday Mass. We look to the word of God to build us up as God's children and community and find strength to use all in the service of God and others in love.

Speak your word O Lord, and we shall be the better for it.

2ND SUNDAY OF LENT

The real Jesus

Things are not always as they seem. Underneath a church that I worked in, are a series of underground passages that go on for about a mile! People are the same – when you are talking to someone and they tell you they are very ill, or recovered from addiction, you see more to them. Or you may find out that someone you thought little of visits an elderly person every week. People are not always as they seem. The mountain visit was the same: the apostles saw Jesus – son of God, radiant in prayer, and in the middle of it all the Passion was announced. They saw the person behind the face.

The big truth of Jesus is that he is intimately united to God the Father. So following him is not just action, but prayer that leads to action. We say someone is a great Christian – he or she helps the poor. Christianity is more – it is also prayer and the Eucharist. While we are thankful for the good lives of many people, we also can say that the full Christian life includes prayer and Mass.

It also involves community – the three were called to witness and help each other remember the Lord Jesus. Community brings the word of God alive in a real way. The community of the Church brings us to fuller faith.

Prayer leads to action for others, and action leads back to prayer. We can be so close to heavenly things that we are no earthly good! Lent brings us into this mystery of the death and resurrection of the Lord – we are part of this, and we try to make life a grace for others. We can transfigure the lives of others, or disfigure. Let's be people of the transfiguration.

Lord show me your face – in myself and in others. Amen.

3ᴿᴰ SUNDAY OF LENT

God of the second chance: The fig tree

This seems a rather strange story about Galileans being killed by Pilate. They were no greater sinners than others, but people thought they were being punished by God. Jesus asks us to repent, but does not punish the sinner. Repent is the word of Lent – and followed by the invitation to believe the good news of the gospel.

A fig tree had three years to get good. It is a precious tree because it uses little water. This one has not produced its fruit. Is God the one to get rid of the tree or the one to give it another chance? God is the God of the second chance all the time.

Never give up on his love! We may need to give God another chance. We know we get angry at times. People find that many good things can happen even in bad times. Let's have that faith and pray for it. God gives us chance after chance in our lives, as He wants our faith in him to grow.

We ask also that we now give the Church another chance. So this is a day of more chances, that life never folds up. We need to return more and more to the gospel and the goodness of so many people, which will lead us in our Church communities to Christ. We do not belittle some terrible things that happened, nor lessen our care for those abused, but ask to take a deeper step to the God who is the one giving and asking us for another chance!

Renew us O Lord, in love, in hope and in joy in your care for us.

4TH SUNDAY OF LENT

Give me the legacy

This is a real family story, about breakups and reconciliation, about love that covers all sorts of happenings and about love to the end. It is about a father who loved all the time, and many a parent identifies with it.

Look at a few things... the son had wanted him dead... *'give me the legacy Da'*. Everyone knew that. He had shamed the family. And the old man waited for years, hoping that his loved son would return.

Look at what happened when he came home – mercy took over – the run, robe, ring and the sandals. He was welcomed as a son. The father doesn't even say once that he forgives. He loves totally and that includes forgiveness.

It's mercy all the time. That repairs the loss. The son wanted to be a hired servant and that would have kept the old man at a distance. He was brought back as a son.

The story is also a call on us to have mercy. People all do wrong – often great wrong. We need a lot of mercy in our country now, but we can't hold bitterness forever. The gospel today encourages us to love as we have been loved with the love that is merciful.

And even when we can't do this – like the elder son – we are still loved. The father says – All I have is yours. God gives his love all the time and waits for our response. Mercy may take time. And God has all the time in the world.

Lord have mercy, on me and on all, today and every day. Amen.

Jn.8:1-11

5TH SUNDAY OF LENT

More than forgiveness

This is a powerful story of justice and mercy. Jesus is on the side of the woman who has been accused of sin and crime. It was an unjust accusation, and the people who brought her had little good in mind.

Jesus offers more than forgiveness – he brings mercy. Mercy forgives with compassion and doesn't read lectures. It restores dignity to the victims of injustice like the lady in this story. It is the same in Jesus, for those who do not receive their dignity because of something they are, or something they did and are unjustly treated.

Jesus did not condemn; he turns the tables a bit. He simply says: *Anyone here without sin – take the stone and throw it.* Nobody does. In this atmosphere of darkness we need to hear something of the love and the mercy of God. Would light of mercy come into their darkness of condemnation? Would they leave their darkness into a personal space where they might have a change of heart?

This is also about the challenge to live honestly and without sin; and to be able to takes steps like this woman's life, to move on. All hear this word from Jesus – *I do not condemn you.* This comes to our society and to ourselves. We need to hear this word for ourselves as often we throw stones at ourselves more than at others. What we condemn in others is what sometimes we do not like in ourselves.

Lord may we enter this world of mercy wherever we need to.
May we hear these words always, 'I do not condemn you.'

PALM SUNDAY

Who was there at the end?

Who was there at the end? The friends of Jesus: from a distance, but still around. They stayed near, not wanting to leave. Did they all stand around for a while? Wanting to go and not wanting to go, like mourners at a graveside – confused, sad and discouraged – silent in the moments of violent death. Were they afraid that this might happen to them too? The friends and acquaintances of Jesus, the one who promised much and said he would rise again… Did any of them remember this promise? Did they whisper it to each other as they closed the stone at the tomb? Did they wonder if more was yet to come? For there was always more with Jesus. We are that 'more'!

There also was the centurion: the good man who said, 'he was a Son of God'. The one from Rome saw through the many from Jerusalem. He was a strange type of guy at the cross – the Roman who had been told to get these crucifixions done, with the least amount of trouble and publicity. Away from home and his own people, he would find a new God in the home of his heart and would be linked forever to a new people.

Something about this man gave a scent of love, and an authority that came from somewhere far away – further than an emperor or a political power. He knew that this man was a Son of God; may we know this too of Jesus.

Lord by your cross and resurrection, you have set us free.
You are the savior of the world.

EASTER SUNDAY

Death is not final

The first Easter parade was just a crowd of women going down the street where once they had sang Hosanna. Another time they had gone with him to death. Now it's just themselves – two Marys, Joanna and other women. The parade was dull, without the one they followed – but they wanted to care for the body with spices, using only the best.

And then it was all different. They saw no body, which frightened them more than any death could have. Then there were angels with strange messages, but their hearts believed quickly and they remembered what he had said. Often, he had talked of death and resurrection. He was the sort of man for whom evil and death could not be final.

They were then to go to the apostles, and they were to find out that caring for Christ's body now would be a different thing. The women announced this divine news to the men. This would have been contrary to the culture at the time, but Jesus went against a lot of beliefs and prejudices.

Caring for the body of Christ now means caring for each other. They would spend the rest of their lives caring for the new body of Christ, and we're the same in caring and being cared for. The risen Christ is in all of us.

We are his body. Not a word of God can be spoken without human words. God reaches us through each other.

The Easter parade now is made up of all of us following our risen Lord, following life that never dies, and the truth of the gospel that can keep us going. This is the love of the risen Lord, which is the lifeblood of the Church.

Jesus Christ you are risen, you are risen indeed, alleluia, alleluia.

2ᴺᴰ SUNDAY OF EASTER

Only faith

Jesus spoke in short sentences and summed up a lot of life in a few words. His final beatitude is in the gospel today – *Blessed are those who have not seen and yet believe*. You can unpack that little phrase and in it you realise that faith is about things that cannot be proved, that it is not easy, and that it brings a blessedness to life. It also includes ourselves – the ones of this year who still believe.

Something is only by faith when everything else fades off. Our loved ones die and only faith assures us that they are alive with God. Only faith assures us that Jesus is present in the mystery of the bread and wine at our Mass. Only faith assures us that he is with us when two or three gather, and only faith assures us that what we do for others we do for him. Faith assures us of some of the best things of life; finally that we come from God and go to God.

Thomas found difficulty with all this. Jesus dealt gently with him, pointing out the wounds of his body and inviting him to touch them. But Thomas never needed to touch the holes in Jesus' hands and feet. He was told that an even better happiness was to believe without touch or sight. He found faith now in the risen Lord, and the faith itself was Jesus' final gift to Thomas.

We need to take time and let faith grow within us. This can be in prayer, in faith-conversation and in allowing ourselves sit quietly and be in the presence of God. In the busy world, this may be difficult, but no day is diminished by time spent in silence and in quiet, knowing we are richly blessed when we grow our faith in God.

Lord, I believe in your presence with me and within me.
Strengthen my belief.

3RD SUNDAY OF EASTER

Tired disciples

Jesus spent time lighting the fire so he could cook breakfast on the seashore. Reminds me of my mother getting the fire ready in the old days so we could make toast with red embers on the long toasting fork. This is Jesus, the risen Jesus. No big apparitions in the sky, but just the simple act in the dawn of cooking bread and fish.

The meal was for tired disciples. Often in the gospel stories he talked about people preparing meals and serving them. He seemed to say a lot through meals and at meals. He allowed a woman dry his feet with her hair at a meal.

In cooking for people love is active. A mother might count up sometime how many meals she has cooked, and call them hours of love. This too is the mission and identity of Jesus.

After death and resurrection comes the Spirit of love. Love given, love received and love shared.

The breakfast meal will end with questions about love. Anything real about the resurrection always ends in being sent by God on the mission of Jesus. He gives little instruction about the mission nor even what it may entail. But it entails being led by God. Life for Jesus is life with Jesus and with the grace of God. We are never alone.

This is the company and the friendship at the source of the life of the soul, and which keeps our unique personality alive. This love comes in prayer and in love and in our loving service of others. This is mission with and for the risen Jesus Christ.

Risen Lord, increase my faith, hope and love.

4TH SUNDAY OF EASTER (VOCATIONS' SUNDAY)

Vocation to compassion

St Ignatius of Loyola had a meditation to offer – that the Divine persons would look down on the world from heaven, and see us all. They had compassion and sent one of them, the Son of the Father, to find us and take us home. That was Jesus, Son of God and son of Mary, divine and human, on a life's mission to guide us to God.

He would do this by his own example and then by leaving the job to us! We are now the ones to be guided and to guide. The good shepherd has made shepherds out of sheep. Only because we are at times lost ourselves can we lead others home. This is the meaning of Vocation Sunday: to take part with God in loving and saving his people and in guiding them at lost times.

People today can get lost in many ways – addictions, pornography, unsatisfying relationships, financial anxiety, suicidal despair. The work of the community of the disciples is to bring the word and the love of God at those points of the journey where we are most lost.

Jesus' heart goes out to all, and especially those in most need, because nobody can steal anyone from God – and nobody can steal God's love from anyone.

The call today is to give as best we can of ourselves in sharing the best of life we have, in sharing love and compassion and knowing that each of us with whatever our talents and goodness are, can partner God in guiding others to him.

May I respond as fully as I can at this time
of my life to your call, O Lord.

Jn.13:31-35

5TH SUNDAY OF EASTER

All are welcome

Where God's glory shines through is in the ordinary – the parent loving the baby, caring for the family, neighbourhood care and concern, the extended family of aunts and uncles who love, the grandparents, and the love of a friend. All this is God's glory – also, in creation like the sunset and the sunrise, the new life of spring and summer. The glory of the divine is in humanity, creation and especially love. The glory of God is humanity fully alive in love, care, compassion and justice.

We can load religion with rules and customs that take on the importance of gospel truths. All are welcome in the house of God and are not to be overburdened with the externals of religion.

A big gospel truth is noted today – love one another. This is our centre – where we come from and where we go to. This is the word for today. In love is God's glory. In the centre of our lives is the love, which is a passion and a motivation.

Love is from God; it shows itself in small ways.

Mass each week brings us back to our centre as does prayer, a good chat with a friend or spouse, time spent doing the good deed for the day or admiring the creation of God.

This makes us share the divine. God became like us that we might become like him. Not alone is God seen in love, but love is seen in God. When we truly love we are truly sharing in the divine life!

Be kind and merciful. Let no one ever come to you without coming away better and happier – Blessed Mother Teresa.

Jn.14:23-29

6TH SUNDAY OF EASTER

God's home

Making a home is a big opportunity of love for a husband and wife and a family. They try to make it their own: pictures and memorabilia here and there make a home out of a house. It doesn't have to be perfect. They want others to be able to feel at home in their home also.

It's the same with Jesus. In our hearts and the depths of our personality he makes a home for himself and the Father. He asks for a loving and welcoming heart, not a place that is perfect, tidy and clean. To make a home is a work of love. Jesus' making of a home in us comes through our growth and development in love. The loving marriage and family, the loving friendship, the heart that cares for others, these are what make Jesus feel at home.

Is this a strange way of looking on God. We think of God in the power of nature and almost the maker of history. God seems to reject this all-powerful view of himself and makes accessible in the home of our hearts.

Home is a place of help. We look out for each other, and the content home is where each cares for the other. St Ignatius used say each day, 'Who can I help today?' Maybe we can make that part of the music of our homes. This is God helping through you, and it is God finding us and each other in love.

Lord, open my heart to prayer and care this day. Open my eyes to the beauty and the problems of others. Open my heart to your love for me.

24:46-53

ASCENSION

God's joy: A new way of being

In the famous crucifix of San Damiano, the Lord ascends with a smile on his face. It is over, his mission is accomplished, and he has conquered death, and is now with us all days to the end of time.

His earthly mission is accomplished, but not his mission of love for his people. He is with us now.

Jesus often talks of joy, often the joy of God in forgiving a sinner. The big joy of God seems to be mercy, and even in the memory of his own death Jesus finds joy. In the chapel of the home of St Francis Xavier in Navarre, the crucifix is of the 'smiling Jesus'. He smiles not in comfort and ease, but in love and sacrifice.

While we think today of the loss of Jesus, we are invited to rejoice as he leaves one way of being with us – on earth, to another way of being with us – from heaven.

He both awaits us there and helps us get there, the mystery of the Divine son who is one of us.

The mystery goes farther; in that we are invited and called into sharing this life of his on earth, for in each of us is the life of Jesus, who makes his home in us.

This is background of the prayer of St Teresa of Avila:
Christ has no body but yours,
No hands, no feet on earth but yours,
yours are the eyes with which he looks
compassion on this world,
yours are the feet with which he walks to do good,
Yours are the hands, with which he blesses all the world...
Christ has no body now on earth but yours.

Jn.14:23-26

PENTECOST SUNDAY

Called into following Christ

Pentecost is really something new! The first reading has no blame, no recrimination for the death of Jesus – only a new call and new mercy. The gospel is about the coming of the Spirit and the main sign of the Spirit is forgiveness.

There was a lot of need for forgiveness around in the first group of Jesus' followers. They had let him down and had let each other down. They looked around and like any group felt memories of hurt, shame, let-down, injury and harm. They saw those who had abandoned Jesus and tried to cover up the sin; or they saw others who just knew they had done wrong and were sorry.

All were forgiven.

And all are now called into the following of Christ. We follow Christ with all sorts of personal gifts, talents and sins in our back-pack. Like people on pilgrimage, we are cluttered. The Holy Spirit opens our hearts to let this baggage just fly away! We are people of freedom and of a new song.

What song do I sing in the presence of the Lord? One that brings me back into misery like singing of shame and misery or one that brings me into the freedom of the Alleluia? Can my heart dance with the joy and hope of Pentecost?

Ask this day for what gift of the Spirit you really want, and maybe include always the gift to be able to let go of hurt, to open the heart to all, and to forgive or if not, to want to forgive.

Holy Spirit, forgiveness of God, give me your true freedom.

TRINITY SUNDAY

Beginning of time – wisdom

Wisdom, truth and love seem to be the themes of readings today, and that love will lead to hope.

It's a confusing sort of feast, as we cannot understand the truth of the Trinity. But we can 'hit' it from different angles.

The wisdom of God has been born before the beginning of time. Somehow wisdom is essential to God – and is presented very often as female. In celebrating the Trinity we celebrate and ask for wisdom, which comes from the heart of God. So this wisdom is the sort of wisdom that comes from love.

Love is 'poured' into our hearts by the Spirit. Connected with love are qualities we would want to live by – courage and hope. These are the gifts of the Spirit as wisdom may be the gift of the Father.

Jesus is presented by the gospel as the source of truth. His also is the truth of love, as his truth is best seen on the cross, in his self-sacrificing love.

The most famous icon of the Trinity by Rugenev, well-known to us now, has the Trinity at a table and an empty space at the table for us all. In one sense they are not completed without us! We are part of their love, and their life of wisdom, truth and love, which they wish to share with us.

Glory be to the Father, and to the Son and to the Holy Spirit.
As it was in the beginning, is now and ever shall be,
world without end. Amen.

BODY AND BLOOD OF CHRIST

Sacrifice and gift

Many people have memories of the Corpus Christ procession when the monstrance with the Blessed Sacrament was brought around the parish. All groups in the parish were represented. Children scattered petals before the host and houses were decorated. The meaning of the feast was to bring the Lord into the streets of his people and to appreciate the gift he gives us of himself in the Eucharist. This procession still takes part in many places.

On Holy Thursday we also celebrate the Eucharist, but in another way. It is more of the sacrifice of Jesus on Calvary. We unite ourselves with his offering that brought him to death, and look forward to the resurrection when the risen Lord would be present in many ways among people, including in the form and shape of bread and wine. On the feast of the Body and Blood of Christ, the emphasis is more on gift than on sacrifice.

This is what he wishes to leave us as a gift forever. It is the way he could give himself forever in a very close way, so that this is his gift of 'food for the journey'

We need this gift. We need to know certainly that God is close with us in life, and the Eucharist at Mass gives us this certainty. We need to know that God is really present in our lives, and we know this in the real presence of the Eucharist.

Lord in this Eucharist today I welcome you into my life;
help me to live like you and love like you. Amen.

Jn.2:1-11

2ND SUNDAY IN ORDINARY TIME

Cana: New wine for life

The human side of the gospel today is the huge need of a young couple on the best day of their lives. Jesus hears of their need and the result is the wine for the wedding, but more so, it is the promise of the fullness of God.

We look for the fullness of life in money, food, sex, travel, security, reputation – none last. Only the simplest joys of life really satisfy in the end, like the joy of love, the thrill of friendship, the caring in family and the ways we enjoy the goodness of creation.

A man asked once in the hospice at the end of his life – 'what is happiness?' 'Find happiness now' was his answer – 'be satisfied, be grateful, for what you have, for what you have received, for what God has given you.' There is a fullness of life in being happy with who I am, what I have... and asking God for what he knows I need.

No matter what our age, we can do good for others, we can share the graces of life and the soul can grow. That's what I hope can happen for me as life goes on. In any group of people, some look happy and some look miserable. The happiest are not always the ones who had or are having the easiest life. They are the ones who have found peace with themselves, others and God.

Because of the gift of the fullness of God in 'new wine', we always have a home, here and after – in the heart of our God in Jesus Christ now and for eternity.

Jesus of the wedding feast of Cana, give us the faith and hope to know
that you can always make a change for the better in our lives,
and the love to live by what we receive.

3RD SUNDAY IN ORDINARY TIME

Faith beyond words

Jesus' religious beliefs grew on the word of God. Through boyhood and family life, visits to the synagogue and prayer, he heard the word of God. Gradually he knew what it meant. Now was his time to speak that word, and to begin his ministry.

For Mary and Joseph this was a proud moment. They had given their time and love to Jesus' upbringing and now it would bear fruit. Today parents worry about the faith of their children. They see a different attitude to religion, prayer, morality and many other aspects of life. They wonder did they do their job well.

Much of the culture today goes against God and religion. Parents cannot fight the culture. But they can hand on the best of the gospel by their own faith and by the way they live their lives, by their love and by speaking the truth as they see it. What is handed on in faith is beyond words.

Teachers and chaplains play a big role in handing on our faith. The Church owes a huge gratitude to teachers, chaplains, priest and lay, who have held that role in very difficult times over the last forty years.

We are all part of the 'faith ministry' of Jesus. By our own prayer we can help a new generation find their way to faith. We hand over worries to the Lord. Prayer gives us the encouragement to support a younger generation in their ways of faith – meditation groups, prayer groups, folk and gospel music Masses, work for and among the poor. God loves our younger generation more than we do!

Lord may my own faith grow deeper by my relationship with you.
Help those who search for you, especially the young.
Help us all to find your love in our lives, Amen.

4TH SUNDAY IN ORDINARY TIME

Christian love

'God, that's very true' – a remark at our liturgy meeting after the second reading. Jealousy kills, envy too, and isn't it great to rejoice in the good fortune of another?

Love is what we bring with us at the end of life. 'We will be judged in the evening of life by love (St John of the Cross). Love for those near and far, for love in the gospel is more than love for just the family, the friend, the attractive one, the neighbour, for all.

There are different calls to Christian love – near and dear daily love, friendship, marriage, relationships. The wider world like in our job where we live in a loving way, in justice with all, not using others for personal gain; the wider world where a universal love makes me want to make a difference in the bigger world. Love carries us into wide seas and waters. It involves us with everyone. It obviously doesn't mean we relate to everyone – nor that we even like everyone. Love is when others' lives become at least as important as our own; and in the deepest loves like marriage, family, and often friendship, others' lives become even more important.

Love changes – we look back and see how the people we loved make the difference. Life is too short to look love in the face and say no. 'We are moulded and remoulded by those who have loved us, and though their love may pass, we are nevertheless their work' (F Mauriac).

The second reading today is hard to beat! We see it in action when we look at the life of Jesus.

> *Jesus whose heart is wide enough to love us all,*
> *make our hearts like yours.*

5TH SUNDAY IN ORDINARY TIME

Christ is alive

Peter got great joy out of being a fisherman, a businessman, with his business partners. Especially when the catch was good and the money was flowing in from Rome and the cities east and west of Galilee.

Jesus offered more – for then, for now and for always. Life to the full was to follow, even in suffering, humiliation and death for Peter.

Christ is alive in love of our family network, our deep friendships, our care for the needy, and our care for the earth. Our volunteers in many places bring the fullness of life of Jesus.

The fish in the story represent all the people who will be found for Christ. And he'd say to Peter, 'look at the fish and think of the people and know that I am alive.'

Sharing and educating in faith is bringing Christ to life. The teachers and chaplains, priests, religious, parish personnel, all educators in faith are in partnership with the Lord Jesus.

All sincere faith knowledge leads to love of God and each other. Conversion is being in love with God and his creation, with each and with everyone. We want to be in a state of love. Only the one who can love can know God, for God is love. That's the challenge to all of us in passing on the faith as best we can to another generation. We pass on our faith in love.

It's not just a catechism but the conviction, belief and joy that Christ is alive. To us Christ would say there will always be fish to be caught and people to be served, the generous gift of God. To us he says there is always love, also the generous gift of God.

Lord, help me to find you in all things,
and then we can do all for your greater glory.

6TH SUNDAY IN ORDINARY TIME

Feeling peace – at the centre of the Beatitudes

On one of my first visits to a Jesuit house, I felt a huge peace – maybe the beginning of a vocation. In bereavement, there can be a moment of peace, which seems to come from nowhere: peace of being totally loved by a good friend or spouse; peace, just peace, with the children.

There is a peace that comes from faith and love, and that is prayer: peace that comes from knowing I am heard, understood and loved.

There is a huge need for listening now, for knowing that people care in our world of suicide and addictions to alcohol. We can feel we live in the impersonal world of anxiety and isolation. We need the peace of honest conversation and openness, and the peace of being forgiven.

Peace is not evading difficulty. You are mad worried about a child – somewhere in the middle, like gold in the mud, you find the peace of knowing God's love for you and for him or her. That needs time and a bit of prayer.

It is good to sit each day in silence. Allow this peace to get into you. Breathe in and out, just saying the word peace. That is God's gift to you. There is also a peace from God in doing good and doing the right thing. Jesus knew it was the best gift he could give. It comes from love.

Back to my first visit that day – what caused the peace? I don't know fully. We can be surprised when we will be graced with the peace of Jesus Christ, which the world cannot give.

Give each of us O Lord, that peace beyond understanding.

7TH SUNDAY IN ORDINARY TIME

Walk in the shoes of each other

A compassionate heart reaches out to many: the gospel today reaches beyond our own circle to reach many others. This will be the constant call of Jesus. When he wants to say what his father is like, he says 'be compassionate like him'.

Compassion is when we can walk in another's shoes, and try to see, hear and feel the world of another, particularly in bad times. It flows from mercy, which is the biggest quality in Jesus.

We like when another can enter into our world without judgement and can accept us in love – Jesus tells us to note this, and then practice the same.

The call is to be compassionate to each other and to the earth! The letter of Pope Francis, *Laudato Si*, calls for a compassionate care of the earth, asking that we hear the cry of the earth, as we hear the cry of the poor; that we treat the earth with the love it deserves.

Compassion for others and for the earth includes our gratitude. We can look deeply into the people we are close to and thank God (and them!) for what we like in them and value. We can look long at creation's beauty in the highest Himalayan mountain and the smallest plant, and recognise that all is the gift of God. We are to care for the earth and till it, and accept the care of the earth for us, giving us food, drink and refreshment. We are to care for each other, and 'till' the lives of each other to bring the best out of each other. This is one of the Pope's central themes about care of creation.

Lord, thank you for the beauty of the earth and of humanity;
may we reverence that beauty for it is from you.

8ᵀᴴ SUNDAY IN ORDINARY TIME

'She must have a lovely heart'!

Someone said to me of a friend – 'she must have a lovely heart'! The gospel today is about goodness inside, and that we draw much from the store of goodness inside ourselves.

A way of looking at this is to wonder what makes us feel positive in ourselves about others, about ourselves and about the world. We have days when we feel truly grateful for much in life and in the world, and the store of goodness fills up. There are days when the opposite happens, and Jesus speaks of the 'store of badness'.

The store of goodness is filled up in many ways – a good conversation with a loved one, time spent with an infant in wonder at how this child is and will be; listening to some good music and admiring good art; taking time for prayer and listening to the word of Jesus in the gospel; finding time to pray with others at the Mass or in prayer groups. God in many ways increases our store of goodness, and we can find ways of allowing this happen. You can find your favourite ways of bringing out the best in yourself.

We know of people we meet whom we always feel the better for meeting. Prayer and faith should also bring the best out of us: give time each day to allow the total love of God for us to reach us.

Another store of goodness is the goodness of self. We can be too critical of ourselves and if so, we will probably find we are critical of others. Look this day into the mirror and give thanks for the man or woman you see there. If we look on ourselves with love, we will look on others the same.

Lord, teach me your goodness.

9TH SUNDAY IN ORDINARY TIME

Less harsh than legalism

Many of us were taught about the division of religion with our long division tables! Catholics and Protestants were deeply suspicious of each other. Doctrines divided, while many shared the heart of religion in prayers and care for the poor. A man of that time once told his bishop that he had gone to a Protestant funeral; the reply was 'well done, and glad you didn't tell me first'. Practice was sometimes less harsh than legalism.

Today's gospel is about friendship, compassion and help that went across Jewish-Gentile divisions, which at the time were very strong. A Roman leader was friendly with the Jewish people to the extent of building the synagogue. This reminds me of many contributions of Dublin Protestants to the building of churches in the years after Catholic Emancipation.

Jesus sees through religious differences to faith. The faith of the man asking for the healing of his servant touched the heart of Jesus. His faith was that Jesus could heal, and he apologised for sending people to ask. He was a humble man; Jesus saw this and the strong faith brought out the healing love of Jesus.

We find faith in many different sorts of places and people. The welcome of the Church to everyone is an essential mark of the Church. It is rooted in the welcoming heart of Jesus.

We might recall also that this Gentile person said words that are repeated at every Mass, as we prepare to receive the Lord. Jesus looks not at our worthiness but at our faith and our sincere efforts to believe.

Lord, I praise and thank you for the gift of my faith;
and for the many people who have helped my faith to grow.

7:11-17

10TH SUNDAY IN ORDINARY TIME

Compassion gives life

Maybe there are two elements to this story about raising the son of a widow to life. It is a sign of the mission of Jesus and fits into the tradition of the prophets. Its source is Jesus' compassion for a widow who has just lost her only son, so that she would not be totally on her own and without support, given that social welfare had not come to that area!

The compassion of Jesus here is so strong that life flows from it into a dead man. The compassion is for someone for whom there would now be little place in society and the fortunes of the widow in that time depended on the religious motivation of the people.

In the end the people were of course amazed, but their amazement brought them to Jesus. We might think that they would be mesmerised by the man raised from death, but their awe brought them to praise God for his great work.

Our ordinary life can bring us in touch with great goodness and spirituality in people, or to a depth of prayer and care for the poor. Through many such people, God is very near and real in the world, and so our praise can be directed to God as we thank these men and women for what they do.

The compassion that flowed from Jesus to bring life to a dead man can flow from us to enliven the lives of others. We can 'grow' this compassion in prayer. Our prayer with God if it is sincere will lead us into the mystery of being loved by God and called into love of others.

Teach us compassion O Lord, for in our compassion for others,
we are doing your will.

11TH SUNDAY IN ORDINARY TIME

A precious gift

Every meal that Jesus shared says something to us about the Eucharist and about Christian community. His 'last supper' was one of many suppers, all of which explains something of who he is and who we are.

At this meal, the one who should have been barred at the door became the principal guest. At Mass all are welcome – the saint and the sinner. The table of the Eucharist would be a circular table, with nobody at the top.

It was a meal of giving something precious of oneself. Her tears were external signs of her real and true self.

We give at Mass – the offertory is the giving of the bread and the wine. With them we give the gifts of the heart at Mass; the love of our lives is poured into the Mass.

And Jesus gives forgiveness and healing. She left the meal better than she came in, and so we too leave Mass better than we came in.

The Mass is one time of giving ourselves as best we can to love and to God. Much of our giving to God is indirect. What we give to others we are giving to God at Mass.

A bright light came into that room when the woman arrived. She brought humility – she knew her place – warmly welcomed by Jesus. The Eucharist is where we are all equal in dignity. Our biggest dignity is we are children of God – she knew that, Simon didn't. She gave of herself, from the heart and God saw that and said things about her that have lasted forever – things he might say of each of us. He loved much; she loved much. And because we are much loved we can love much in return.

Lord may I love in life what you love.

12TH SUNDAY IN ORDINARY TIME

Jesus making sense

Taking up a cross – a theme of Jesus. The cross will be the destiny of Jesus, but not the end. It will be love to the end but not the end of his life among us. We are people always with a future, because of Jesus who is alive now. Do we really believe this?

The road of God is like the road of Jesus. On it we find companionship with like-minded people, we find love and joy, and we find the cross. We are to take up the cross daily, which means we are to accept as best we can the trials and troubles that life sends us. God is with us in this.

We find his help in the example of Jesus. He often told his followers that he would suffer, be crucified and be put to death. They did not believe this, and neither did they remember that he promised he would rise from the dead.

Only when we accept and enter into the cross of life will we know the real hope that comes from following the Lord Jesus.

In the middle of the darkness is the light. Each of us finds Jesus in our own lights and darkness, as his word reaches out to us there.

There is the cross of following him, which leads many today to torture and death. We pray in solidarity with them.

The cross – should it have a figure? It should be empty with the triumph of the resurrection. The first crucifixes had on them the risen Christ. He will suffer and enter into his glory. The end is never what we think it is. Everything in life can lead to Jesus, and he brings everything in life into his light.

Lord, in your light, we see light. May we trust always in your light.

13TH SUNDAY IN ORDINARY TIME

Dramatic examples

There's something about consistency that we like. We like people to follow through what they say and what they believe in. We mistrust promises that are made with hidden agendas and meanings, like most political promises. Jesus has a similar view and in storing images this Sunday he asks for consistency. If we are to follow him then property (where to lay one's head), family (burying one's father) and relationships (saying goodbye), while important and relevant, are secondary.

These may sound very tough, like a demand not to go to a parent's funeral; Jesus wishes them to be put in context of honouring our parents also, but he uses them as dramatic examples of following in his path. Following him is a decision, not just a feeling.

These were said to people who wanted to follow him, who had found a desire to live as he asked. This is a great grace. Can we be grateful for the loving call of God to follow his way of life?

It can give a great meaning to life, and an added meaning to marriage, love, parenthood and jobs. Jesus is asking that we place real and sincere love at the top of our priorities. Our love for him and our commitments in love and faithfulness are sides of the one coin.

This will bring the greatest happiness possible – to live in love and for love, in the big and the ordinary ways of life. How often we can be really happy at the end of the day for what we did that helped others.

Lord, teach me to love as you do, to remain true to others and to you.
May your kingdom come in your people.

10:1-12, 17-20

14TH SUNDAY IN ORDINARY TIME

Hand over to God

In the smallest of the details of our love and the biggest God is near. God is near with love and also with care. We might think of it as a powerful care – power not for himself but for us.

God's Power enables us to do what we can't do ourselves, like people in AA who hand their lives over to the higher power each day. Sometimes we find when we are at our lowest God is at his strongest in our lives. Augustine wrote that when we love ourselves least, God loves us most.

Where do we find him, or rather where does God find us? God is present in all things – we don't have to go to Church or read the bible to find God, as God is present to us in many ways. God is in all of creation – love and friendship, a sunset or sunrise. His hand is in our food and drink, our work, study, reflection and insights. He is ever present in our efforts to live well, to stay clean of drugs, alcohol or crime. God is in the midst of real life and in the centre of the soul is a space where nobody can enter without our welcome and invitation, and where God dwells.

When we see Jesus in action we know the kingdom is very near.

At Christmas we welcomed the kingdom, in the love for the poor, in the miracle of human birth.

At Easter we welcomed the kingdom as the place of eternity, of victory over death and pain, of justice over injustice. All the time welcoming the kingdom whose real power is love and whose hope still today is the coming of justice and peace.

Lord may your kingdom come and your will be done on Earth.

15TH SUNDAY IN ORDINARY TIME

The teller of the story

Is this the best story ever written! Because we know it so well, we may gloss over it. It challenges us on many levels – the inclusiveness of everyone as our neighbour; the way we can pass by human needs, and how the most rejected people can respond positively. It is a story of how many of us miss tragedy under our noses, and how many suffer because of the cruelty of others. It's mainly a story to ask us to respond as positively as we can to all human need.

It also points to the person who told the story. Jesus could tell this story because he was the good Samaritan himself. His heart went out to those who were suffering most at the hands of others. He could tell it also because he knew what it was like to be an outcast – rejected by his own people, and in danger all the time of being victimised even to death like this man at the side of the road.

He brings it farther also – saying that the commandment of God is seen in the way the good Samaritan responded. The second great commandment is to love the neighbour, and the neighbour is the one of any colour, nationality, age or family.

We can ask who are the ones thrown to the side of the road today? The former prisoner, the asylum seeker and refugee, the forgotten young person, the addict, among others. All can be helped to their feet and to carry on in life through the help and care of another.

The final words to take from the gospel today are simple yet difficult – 'go and do the same yourself'.

Lord, may I go and do the same myself.

10:38-42

16TH SUNDAY IN ORDINARY TIME

Jesus and hospitality: God's footprints

The half door on the old Irish house had many functions. It kept the animals out while allowing the family to look out. It also made for openness and hospitality for all who passed by. The traveller was welcomed and the one walking by could rest for a while. We were open to the world and the world to us, and we felt safe.

Hospitality was important in Jesus' time. He made many a visit to the house of Martha and Mary, staying there when he wanted to go to Jerusalem. They enjoyed having him – Mary just sat there listening to him – the stranger, now a friend, who told stories of how life could best be lived. I can imagine him telling the parables in their house.

The people then had a belief in the travelling and pilgrim God, the one who came our way often. The first reading is about strangers being entertained and the people didn't know that the Lord was visiting them. When we open our heart and home to the stranger and to the neighbour we are receiving God into our lives.

The Indian poet Tagore writes – *'and when you left I saw God's footprints on the floor.'*

Our fear of break-ins and of robbery today is destroying an easy accessibility in our neighbourhoods. Casual hospitality is more difficult than in the days of the half-door. Maybe Facebook and Twitter and other social media fulfil some of this function, impersonal though it may be. We cannot live in isolation. 'Self knows that self is not enough' writes the poet, Brendan Kennelly.

For friendship and love, especially when I find it in unexpected places and people, thank you, Lord.

17TH SUNDAY IN ORDINARY TIME

Trust in prayer

Often I pray to St Anthony and I find what I was looking for. I can't understand why, but it brings up the question of praying for what we want and need. People pray hard for an intention; some pray for ages and are answered, some are not.

We often pray for what may be outside God's control: that someone may give up drink, when the person may not want to; that children will be kept safe on the roads, but they are killed or injured with the careless and dangerous driving of someone else, maybe under addictive influence.

We are encouraged always to pray with hope and persistence, believing that we always get something. In the asking is the receiving, and we never leave prayer worse off than when we began.

For any time we give to prayer, we get something. We are transformed. St Ignatius speaks of the effect of prayer – an increase in faith, hope and love. We may not get the specific intention but we always get the Holy Spirit. I have never left prayer the poorer than when I began. In the knocking at the door itself something is opened. In asking and seeking we get something. The first gift of prayer is the love of God. Other gifts follow.

Prayer increases our trust in God, that he wants our good and is with us in love.

So we pray for what we need and then leave the prayer with God, to be answered as he can. This is one of the greatest faiths of all.

Our Father, holy be your name, your kingdom come and will be done within me and in earth and heaven.

18TH SUNDAY IN ORDINARY TIME

Rich in whose sight? – Love not wealth

You can look around a lot and the gospel today makes sense. It points at how we can get caught up in what we own and what people have. It's about possessions and how they take us over – or how we react when we lack what we once had. We enjoy wealth but we have a mixed reaction to it.

Saint Ignatius mentioned three obstacles to our faith – wealth, honour, pride. He saw from his own experience that people wanted wealth so that they would be highly thought of – it can be the right school, the right address, the right bank. We have pride in what we have, but as we know, things can change very quickly. Shares go down; you may become ill or die.

The battle is between being rich in the sight of the world and being rich in the sight of God.

The opposites of these obstacles are simplicity, integrity, and humility. Humility is pride in who we are – children of God, brothers and sisters to each other, and accepting ourselves just as we are. We need nothing outside of ourselves to make us feel good about ourselves. This too is simplicity.

What we have is a gift, given to us for the good of the world, the community, the neighbourhood, not just for the good of the self.

And in the end, what matters is that we are judged on love not on wealth. Or if we have had wealth, we will be judged on what we did with it. It can lead us away from God very easily. Do we live like him? Be rich in God – in mercy, love, forgiveness and justice.

Lord, may your kingdom of justice and peace come on earth.

19TH SUNDAY IN ORDINARY TIME

Looking after his business

When you go away and want someone to mind the house, you plan well and invest in someone safe. We often need that. Who will monitor the alarm and keep an eye on the house?

Same with Jesus... the people of the gospel are the ones who look after his business while he is away! God invests in us. He wants us to do our best in minding his house. His community and Church are the people to whom he entrusts his life's work.

We spread the kingdom in simple ways every day – care, hospitality, work for justice, compassion, with the gifts and talents we have. He has given us the gifts – we are to use them in his service. We do our best and God, the architect, is continually building with us.

He is the extra presence around in his Spirit. So when we do things in his service, he is the inspirer. But he leaves a lot to us.

And then when in his service he feeds us. He works with us and for us. The slave/master relationship is turned upside down. People would never expect that the master would serve the meal – like at the washing of the feet. We are nourished and renewed.

There is a need now for volunteer help within the Church – we need it now and will in the future. Formation is needed for people who can hand on faith when the parish may be called on to do more, and to do what the Catholic school has done until now.

The kingdom is spread through the work of the Church, and we are this Church, this body of Christ. We are the true blessed sacraments of Jesus Christ.

Lord, may your kingdom come.

20TH SUNDAY IN ORDINARY TIME

Disturbing love and the warmth of love

Fire is frightening; it can burn up a city. Controlled it is warming: in control in a grate; and it also warms the heart, when we sit back, watch the flames and chat, think or pray. Jesus came to bring fire on the earth.

His is the warmth of love and companionship: when we know we can go to him just as we are, and enjoy the intimacy of his friendship – the friend who is always offering the gift of his heart to each of us.

The warmth of Jesus brings comfort and hope to the world when we live in isolation from each other, lack of friendship and hope. When we lack the reconciliation and justice that makes life possible among us, then the warmth of God's love for all can inflame our coldness.

There is also the fire that disturbs; love challenges as well as comforts. The flame of God can be frightening in that it demands a world of justice, peace and reconciliation. The fire of this love is the fire that also warms and comforts.

The flame of God is the Holy Spirit. Jesus comes to bring all sorts of fire to the world, and to send the Spirit of comfort, justice, reconciliation and hope. The message of Jesus may divide us, and if it does, the love of Jesus can unite us, for love is the most powerful gift of Jesus.

A saying has it – he has come to afflict the comfortable and comfort the afflicted.

Holy Spirit, flame of God, hover over each of us as you did
for the followers of Jesus at the first Pentecost.

21ST SUNDAY IN ORDINARY TIME

World of love

In a family so much love is lavished on the new-born first child, and you hear them saying that's the end of freedom now for a good few years. Or the grandchildren come and there's the babysitting. Life deepens love and narrows our freedom. Jesus says elsewhere that love is the door to eternal life. In laying down life for a friend, the cross was a narrow door.

Real love means little things a lot of the time, and with God it means time now and then dedicated to prayer and to worship, as well as loving our neighbour.

Love demands a lot as well as giving a lot. With the people we most love, we are most vulnerable and they can bring the worst and the best out in us.

The sick child, the elderly in the family, those in prison or in a difficult marriage call on our love, as does a husband or wife needing a lot of care in illness or old age. There is a special love shown by volunteers in our country and the developing world. The grandchild who is isolated and lonely calls too on our love. This is the world of love, the only world worth sacrificing anything for.

The condition for entering is not where you come from, whether you are first or last, whether you wear the right clothes or even turn up on time – the condition is that, in the way of the living God, you hear the word of God daily and live by it faithfully.

Lord, may your will of love be done on Earth.

22ND SUNDAY IN ORDINARY TIME

Strange ways

A fellow said – 'bad enough he was in the pub, but now I have to be beside him at Mass'. Said jocosely, but the point is that everyone is invited to the banquet of Jesus like the gospel today. We never know who we might meet at Mass.

Jesus has strange ways of looking on whom to invite and who are the most important.

There were strict codes of place-names and seating at this type of party. Jesus was going to cut through these. He also had upset things earlier by healing a very sick man on the Sabbath. He started talking then about who to invite.

There was no pecking order at his invitation. The narrow door of last week has been pushed wide to let them all in.

The community of Christ doesn't admit of differences that put us down. He was always saying this, and saying it to the proud and haughty. For others, life had taught them to be humble and they could probably enjoy this feast.

Humble people are grateful for small and big things; they pray often and know their need for prayer; they know they have faults and are no better or worse than most, and know they need God's mercy; they love children because they are childlike at times, and they know they are not humble all the time. They don't take themselves too seriously and are compassionate to the faults of others. They know who they are – in one way the least of all, but always loved, always forgiven, always a child of God.

Lord, teach me to know myself well,
so that I can better know your love.

23RD SUNDAY IN ORDINARY TIME

Created Good

Giving up possessions is a huge demand of Jesus. It can be misunderstood and cause grief. What Jesus means is that we identify what it is in us that may block us being his disciples. Wealth may provide comfort, status in society or the Church, security, or whatever centres our concerns, and whatever keeps us from acting justly with and for others.

Created in the likeness of God, we are created good. In each of us is the desire to nourish what is good and best in us. We wish to do the same for our children, our pupils or anyone in our care.

We nourish the good in ourselves by prayer, community, by good deeds and an honourable way of life. We watch the example of Jesus and listen to how he teaches us in his stories. Today he asks us to know ourselves, just like the man building a tower plans what he has and what he can do.

Our goodness in life is a gift from God. We find goodness also in each other. Good people make good people better! Saints we like show us a way to God and inspire us, and even help us. The gospel is full of people trying to do their best and learning with fresh starts and after their mistakes how to follow Jesus.

Goodness is vulnerable. We can try our best and fail. We make promises that don't last despite our best efforts. In the eyes of God goodness is in what we do and in what we try to do. God sees the goodness of the heart.

Lord give us a desire for the good in our lives
and help us live by your good gospel.

24TH SUNDAY IN ORDINARY TIME

No accidents of birth

The lost coin was a precious coin to the lady in question in the gospel. The coin would have been part of her dowry, which with the other nine coins would have been made into a crown she wore on her head. So all could see now that her crown was flawed and a bit of mockery and fun might follow. Jesus knew when he told the story that it would reach the heart.

He would also know that people might make the connection – as every coin was essential to the crown, so we are all valued and essential to God. There are no accidents of birth, and nobody excluded from the promise of life forever with God.

The woman would go to great efforts to find the lost coin. Jesus went to great efforts to save each of us, even to crucifixion and death. We are worth the death of God, and are now the joy of God's life, like a child to a parent, and like the joy of friends to each other.

Even the first reading has God loving his people with heartfelt love. He is angry with them for a while but this anger is mixed with love and his love wins in the end.

The love of God is an active love, reaching to us in mercy and forgiveness, always building us up. This searching for all his people in mercy is the most characteristic quality of God, if we can put it so humanly. We are all children – on each birth and baptismal certificate, we can write a second father's name – God!

Father, create us anew each day in Jesus, your Son.

Amos 8:4-7

25TH SUNDAY IN ORDINARY TIME

On the side of the poor (first reading)

Isn't it still the same as the first reading has it? The poor get the worst of things, and are diddled; it's quite contemporary. It is about greed and fooling the poor; raising the shekel – like raising the exchange rate so that the poorer countries get less dollars for their kwacha and rupees; golden handshakes for people whose greed is palpable and whose attitudes have left so many people hard up; money well protected and taxes avoided if not evaded. Our waste of food could feed so many. People are poor not through their own fault but because they are neglected.

How many of the poorer schools are becoming less well off, with resources such as special needs assistants taken away. Hospital care is getting worse, as people wait for prolonged periods for treatment. Mostly the poor will first suffer from economic mishap. God hates this – he hates mistreatment of his people. Jesus raged against the exploitation of the poor.

We pay tribute to the people who work for the poor and needy – in the parish; in diocesan and other social agencies, and our volunteers at home and abroad. Can we vote for public representatives who care for the poor?

The call to the Church is to care as Jesus cared; we need the harsh words of the first reading sometimes to waken us up, and the story of Jesus to make sure we don't sleep again.

Pope Francis said: 'if investments in banks drop a little, it's a tragedy!
But if people are starving, if they have nothing to eat, if they are not
healthy, it does not matter! This is our crisis today!'
Lord, may your kingdom come!

26TH SUNDAY IN ORDINARY TIME

Faith in action: On fire with hope

This story of Jesus highlights the inequality of rich and poor. Jesus appeals to our sense of justice, right and goodness. There is no need for anyone to come back from the dead to warn us of this inequality. The doors between rich and poor can often be locked as were the doors between Dives and Lazarus. Those outside can only knock, protest and even break down doors. The doors must be opened from the inside.

This message of justice and hope for an equal share of the world's goods for everyone is strong in the gospel of Jesus. His heart was on fire with the hope of a better life for the poor. He went to help them simply because they were poor.

The Christian Church, if it is to be faithful to the gospel, should be involved in many ways in the creation of a more just world. The Christian parish takes a special care for the refugee, the new poor, the unborn, the elderly, and in fact all whose voices may not be usually heard.

The parable is meant not to scare with images of punishment, but to make us as aware of the huge inequalities that exist in our world, and in the exploitation of resources in the developing world.

Maybe we can pray not to be tormented by any of the pains of this story, but be tormented into action by the hunger, poverty and injustices of our world. Maybe then more doors can be opened from the inside of wealth to the outside of poverty.

Lord, may we build with you a world of justice and peace.

27TH SUNDAY IN ORDINARY TIME

Gift of faith

Interesting that Jesus says we don't need much faith – only the size of a mustard seed, the smallest of all seeds in his time. Does he really mean this?

He seems to be saying that faith does not depend on us. It is a gift from God, which grows throughout our lives, 'fanned into a flame', as in the second reading. We need to have confidence in the faith we have rather than always berating ourselves that it is little. In the Christian parish and community there is often more faith than we realise.

In a parish we have the people who serve the sick and the poor; those who pray a lot and those who worship; those who reflect on faith and question. There are the families where faith is expressed in many different ways. Every moment where we come in touch with the world beyond ourselves, whether directly religious or not, is a moment of faith.

We can trace the history of our own faith and remember personal moments that strengthened the faith. These can be varied – prayer, love, works of justice, the beauty of creation, times of illness and death, sacramental life. What is important is that they are personal moments between us and God, which are privileged times of the growth of the mustard seed of faith.

We need the faith community. We need to work together for the just world recognised in the first reading as the prophet 'denounces violence, contention and discord.' We need the leadership of the community, clerical and lay, to point out ways of faith for our culture and our times. In this way God grows the mustard seed, which is the beginning of faith.

In the end faith grows in surprising ways. God is at work all the time, supporting our faith in varied and heartfelt ways.

Lord, I believe, strengthen my belief.

28TH SUNDAY IN ORDINARY TIME

A grateful heart

Nine were cured, and a tenth was healed. The last one came back and lifted his heart in praise and thanks.

He was a man of another country, not liked by the followers of Jesus, yet his heart was like the heart of Jesus, thankful and light.

The word 'thanks' can change an atmosphere. It is one of the most important words between people who are in ordinary and consistent relationships. With those we love, with those with whom we work, live, and with whom life is shared, it is a word that deepens the bond among us. It brings lightness among us.

The Christian heart is a grateful heart. We sometimes find people whose lives are very difficult and disabled on the outside but have a heart of thanks on the inside. They are the people who give thanks for what they have, rather than whine over what they have not.

The thanks of the Samaritan brought him into a sort of unity with Jesus and with the others who looked on him as a foreigner. Thanks can bring enemies together. When we give thanks for the same things, we shatter barriers.

The nine were cured, and probably did well for Jesus in their reports. But the tenth brought the new life of Jesus to others from a grateful heart.

Give thanks this day for the ordinary, for the people who are always there, for the goodness of God. Give thanks, and in giving thanks we will be more like Jesus, the one whose life and words thank God his Father.

Lord Jesus it is right to give you thanks and praise.

29TH SUNDAY IN ORDINARY TIME

People with backbone

We like people with backbone, the courage of their convictions; who follow through on what they say they will do; who are not wishy-washy. Jesus was like that.

He feels a fire in his heart, in his belly and he wants it to be lit. The fire is the fire of justice – wanting the justice this widow was due. The job of the judge at that time was to care for the widow and orphan, the neglected ones of society. She had a right to his assistance.

What he stands for, the Church stands for, even with opposition. This is a culture that supports life at all stages; which speaks out against any injustice; which supports love and wants to encourage relationships of real and genuine love. Its views on sexuality and sexual relationships will mirror that, in a world where sex can be very casually viewed and used. The Church supports the elderly, and a culture of sharing rather than accumulation of wealth; works and supports peace in the world; and joins in the fire of Jesus to bring the reign of God alive in the world.

The fire of Jesus is the fire of love, compassion and justice – three core values of the Christian and of the Church. We need to keep all that alive and not get caught up in administration and buildings, even overriding regrets about the past.

Can we hope that we can be a Church that fulfils and makes alive the best of the fire of Jesus? He 'has come to bring fire to the earth' and wants it to be kindled.

Lord, may your kingdom come.

30ᵀᴴ SUNDAY IN ORDINARY TIME

The Pharisee's boast

This is one of these stories of people who didn't like each other, and brought the worst out of each other. The Pharisee was strict on religion, and the tax man was a greedy sinner. Each made the other feel awful about themselves, especially before God.

The Pharisee started boasting about his religious fervent observance. The tax man just swallowed his prejudice and admitted to God that he was a sinner. The Pharisee would look good in any religious line-up, and the tax man would be in the corner of the line-up, almost cowering in the back of the prayer-place, hoping nobody would see him.

But he knew who he was before God; he admitted his weakness. The Pharisee pretended religious fervour and looked down on the tax man, one of God's favourites.

Jesus comments on the story that everyone would recognise, and we recognise ourselves in both people: the proud and arrogant person at times, and at other times, the one who feels a total failure.

He just says – in admitting who you are, you are high in the sight of God and high at God's table.

Just to be oneself before God can be difficult. Many gospel stories are about this reality. We need to give those few silent moments each day to an awareness of being loved by God. In that we are humbled, that one as good as God could love us so totally, and so we are exalted.

We are gifted by God's grace and if we can enjoy our identity as a child of God we will find happiness in life.

Lord teach me to know you more,
to love you more and serve you faithfully in my life.

19:1-10

31ST SUNDAY IN ORDINARY TIME

Made to belong and to share

In the presence of Jesus, Zacchaeus, the little man with a big story, found out who he really was and what he was made for. That's the way it is with Jesus.

His big story wasn't impressive. The whole town knew of his corruption and his exploitation. Many could tell a story of being diddled by him into paying more tax than was just. He carried this burden all the time and somehow the arrival of Jesus impelled him to climb a tree so that his life would be changed. Our stories are all a mixture of good and evil. We carry burdens of guilt and sin and hurt and anger. We need to get free and be the self we can be.

He found he wasn't the mean person he had been showing all his life. He found that restoration of ill-gotten gains, and a promise to help his neighbour, would bring more happiness than his past. He found in meeting Jesus the acceptance that allowed him to change, to go public on his change, and to continue a changed life no matter what others thought.

He was made for community, belonging and sharing; not for isolation, loneliness and greed. He knew now he was made for love for he found himself loved by God in Jesus, so that the one everyone was talking about visited his house now.

It didn't make Jesus popular. They blamed him for going to the house of someone like that. It's often like that; we would like Jesus to look down on the ones we look down on. The only time Jesus looks down on us is from his cross – to raise us up to the heights of love and humanity we are made for.

Lord Jesus we are made in your image;
help us to live in your likeness.

32ᴺᴰ SUNDAY IN ORDINARY TIME

A new breakthrough

Big question of what it will all be like? Jesus gives no details. We live in hope and die in hope. We are to be alive forever in the love of God. God keeps love safe. When life ceases, love stays.

God is God of life, the Gospel says; 'to him all are alive,' even the dead.

God breaks into life in a new way at our death. It happens in small ways every time we are transformed a bit – when we forgive, make peace, really help another, when we promise ourselves to someone or some cause, we are in resurrection-mode. But the final one is a gift unlike any earthly gift.

We need to share this hope with each other. The peace you may have felt at the death of someone, the dream where the loved one was happy, the thanks you feel for another for ever – all brings hope even if their death is sudden or self inflicted or at a young age. As we place our candle at the altar for our loved ones in November, we are letting them go off into what death really is – our finding our way to the arms of God.

Words of Pope Francis – 'Hope is not looking at a half-full glass, which is simply optimism, which is a human attitude that depends on many things. Hope is a gift of Jesus, of His very self, His very name is hope. It is Christ in you, the hope for glory.'

This is the eternal hope, which is the root of our joy even in the losses of our lives.

Lord, give us this day a renewal of faith in eternal life.

33RD SUNDAY IN ORDINARY TIME

The feet of the sun

The imagery of the readings is frightening and cannot be easily understood. Maybe one aspect is of the contrasts we live with – terror and violence among ourselves and the Earth, and also the healing and gentle power of God. 'The sun of justice will shine with healing in its rays'. When we see the terrors of the globe, it is a sign that God's power is also in our midst: 'do not be frightened', we are told.

If you look at the sun in the evening, you often see the rays of light hitting the Earth. In Irish they are called *'cosa na gréinne'* – the feet of the sun. We can think of them as God's feet walking along our scorched and wounded earth: through the poverty and the illness of his world, through fields full of landmines and unexploded bombs, the rays of light take their pilgrimage from heaven through our world, which needs the light of God so badly.

Even in persecution the presence of God is near. Even in betrayal and in the conflicts that arise over the word of God and how to live the gospel, God is near. He never abandons his people. We can almost sum up the message of the prophets as 'God does not abandon us'.

In years when the Church throughout the world was stripped of almost all except its relationship with Jesus, we know that despite the faults, sins and weaknesses and the huge need for renewal, God is near in the word of Jesus Christ. It is in listening to his word and interpreting it together for today that we will find our true way forward as his community.

Lord Jesus, may your kingdom come
and your will be done on earth as in heaven.

FEAST OF CHRIST THE KING

Jesus couldn't do much for the man on the cross... his own hands were nailed. He couldn't take him off, but he gave him more than he could ask for. He gave him paradise.

Where is God in our suffering? What sort of hope can we find this week in our country? What with so many horrible atrocities taking place, and the economic mess we have. What has God and the Church to say? God in his love for his people, and the Church with its social teachings – have they any message of hope?

Where is God? God did not cause the recession nor murders. We may learn a lot through it and good may come later or now. Our suffering at the moment is of human making. Not of our making, but of some of our leaders and bankers, mostly through greed. God is with us suffering like he was with the thief. He didn't cause the suffering of the man on the next cross to him. He wants our happiness and wants justice and prosperity for all.

God is with us, holding our hands, asking us to support each other. The Church will offer a place and space to find the love of God, and its social teaching will ask us to look for the common good in the future. It offers also a place where we can hear the Church's approach to our economic future, reminding us all the time of the needs of the poor and the ordinary in education, medical care, housing and the ways in which the very old and the poor will suffer most in a situation which has been none of their doing. We are the Church and called on to make our voices heard for those who, like the man on the next cross, have little voice except to ask for help.

Lord, thy kingdom come.

MISSION SUNDAY

A passionate spirit

Irish people have long memories of helping the missions – collecting stamps, mission groups in schools, maybe aunts and uncles 'out foreign'. It is an essential part of the Church, because Christ is missionary, sent not just to one, but to all, to make a better world, founded on the gospel of Christ. Even if people are not baptised, the Church wants to point out the way to a truly human life – in the way, truth and life who is Christ, and committed to the world of justice.

With so much hunger, ill health, and lack of education, the missionary spirit is passionate about wanting to improve things with the message of the gospel.

Today we pray for our missionaries. They are helped by our prayers in what is often a lonely life for them. Help the missionary societies if we can; think of giving some time in volunteering in the poorer world; decide to vote for people who are concerned for the developing world and who will maintain our aid to the world in need; and we can encourage the young to think globally.

We pray for courage for our people overseas and also for ourselves that we can live as Jesus in different ways. All are missionaries as Pope Francis says – 'Each individual Christian and every community is missionary to the extent that they bring to others and live the Gospel, and testify to God's love for all, especially those experiencing difficulties. Be missionaries of God's love and tenderness! Be missionaries of God's mercy, which always forgives us, always awaits us and loves us dearly.'

May our lives be lived in love and service of you,
Lord God, and of each other.

Mt.2:1-12

FEAST OF THE EPIPHANY

Gifts say something about the person who gives the gift, as well as their view of the person receiving. The Magi's gifts say something about their faith, their trust and their knowledge of who Jesus would be.

Gold was for a king; frankincense for someone divine and myrrh for the anointing at death. The gifts say a lot about Jesus – God and man, and he would die and be entombed.

For us now, the only gift worth our giving is our love. We bring love and ask God to accept the love of our lives – husband and wife, children, friends, neighbours: whoever are the loves of life we can bring to the crib today.

But there is another gift. The biggest gift of today is the child in the crib – God's gift to humanity. He knows what we need. And we need Jesus' message in our country – to address the lack of respect for life, the violence on our streets, abuse of alcohol, our use of others for comfort, pleasure, wealth – there are many ways we harm each other. There is also a lack of faith and meaning in life.

Deep down the gift of God today is of love for us; and the invitation to let this love flow into our lives and our society, so that we live as God asks us to live.

Can we go to the crib and just offer ourselves and our love this day?

We call today 'little Christmas'. Can we with our love make little Christmas a really big Christmas, and make each day of the year a gift of love to the Lord.

Christ-child, may your love fill the earth.

5:1-11

MARCH 17TH ST PATRICK'S DAY

Liking or hating St Patrick's Day!

Part of me dislikes St Patrick's Day. I fear it has been taken over by a cultural celebration with no reference to the spiritual or the faith side of the saint. We'll see all sorts of funny St Patricks, a cultural pageant, often lovely in itself. But have we forgotten the meaning and kept the man? He would hardly recognise his feast himself.

To understand Patrick, we must see the place Christ had in his life. Saint Patrick looked to the Christ of the Gospels for his inspiration. As a young boy he was imprisoned on Slemish Mountain, away from home, like many of our people in the past and our foreign people today. In prayer to Christ he felt secure and strong. His *Confessions* reveals how that security and strength came from a Christ centered spirituality.

To our young people, Patrick has a message – you can get to know Christ when you are young. He is the friend of young and old. Religion is not something just for old age and when death is around. You can have big dreams and they can involve a big world, willing to give what you are and who you are for God. He is the original youthful pilgrim – his 'camino' of Ireland brings us from Mayo to Slane to Tara to Donegal and the little holy wells of Patrick all over the country. His pilgrimage brings us into the life of the people and the life of God.

May Christ be with us!
May Christ be before us!
May Christ be in us,
Christ be over all!
May Thy Grace, Lord,
Always be ours,
This day, O Lord, and forevermore. Amen.

AUGUST 15ᵀᴴ FEAST OF THE ASSUMPTION

The talking Mary

There are people who talk all the time. You or I could be one of them and not realise it. Maybe it is just exuberance of personality, or a brain packed full of ideas that simply must poke their way out. Mary is a silent woman in the gospel. But today's reading is different.

Why does the newly pregnant Mary talk so much this Sunday? She has hurried to her cousin Elizabeth's house in the hill country, and hardly have they even said hello when Mary bursts into a long speech or song, the one we traditionally call the *Magnificat*. In it she even says that all generations are going to call her blessed – talking about herself, so it seems.

Not really! Mary is actually responding to what Elizabeth has just said. 'You are the mother of my Lord! Blessed are you who believed that what was spoken to you by the Lord would be fulfilled.'

In return Mary lets excited words pour from her mouth. But the *Magnificat* is not about Mary; it is entirely about God. She will be blessed by all generations, she says, not at all because she is herself something great, but because God's love and mercy are great, and they will pour out through her to the world.

The feast of the Assumption salutes Mary's trust and openness. She had been at one with God all her life, even in the searing passion and death of her son. Faith in her Assumption is an acknowledgment of how close she had been to Jesus all life long, and especially in his death. It is faith that she is body and soul in heaven.

Pray for us Mary, now and always.

Mt.5:1-12

NOVEMBER 1ˢᵀ ALL SAINTS

Called to be holy

'So and so is a bit of a saint!' What do we mean by saying this?

Saints were people who were close to God. We venerate them and name them. We pray to them and are inspired by them.

The gospel gives another clue to why they were saints – the qualities of their lives.

Called to be holy those who mourn... people who are really good – merciful; peacemakers; and hunger for justice. Nothing about prayer – this is understood and their lives come from prayer. But the qualities of a saint are human qualities we really like.

A saint is a person close to God in prayer and from this centre comes his or her service of people. Someone may do the same work as a saint but not be a saint.

People love to meet a real saint – they bring out the best in us, not remind us of the worst!

We can extend our feast today to salute all the unknown saints we have met.

We are called to be holy in a human way. A saint is not a perfect human being, but one who has brought his or her life totally to God and becomes human in a way of love, compassion and care for all.

Pope Francis says: The feasts of All Saints and All Souls are 'days of hope,' he said: 'There are difficult moments in life, but with hope you go forward and keep your eyes on what awaits us. Today is a day of hope; our brothers and sisters are in the presence of God, and we, too, will be there in the Lord's arms if we follow the path of Jesus.'

Saints of this parish – pray for us.

DECEMBER 8TH
FEAST OF THE IMMACULATE CONCEPTION

Full of grace: Gifts of grace at birth

A child with a bad temper – just like his father, we might say. Likes her food, just like her mother, always. Could buy and sell you with words, like her grandmother. We can see the delights and the faults of a parent in a child. We pick up some personality strengths and faults at birth. Mary was different – she had nothing of the sin, badness or evil that all are born with. By grace of God Mary picked up none of the faults of her parents or the sin we are all born into.

What we will be like in the future – the brightness and light of God with all sin gone, she got at conception as grace. This because of what her son would be and do.

Puts her different... in one way yes. But on another she can really understand us. Truly good people seem to be able to see through you with love. They never condemn. We don't mind that they know our faults. Mary lived in total goodness, and that means she can see goodness where others might not.

Grace meant that she could see God in all things. No blocks of sin and selfishness. In the little and the great, Mary and God were one. In love she knew the love of God, in the beauty she saw, she saw the beauty of God, in all of life God was near to her.

The grace of today's feast kept her going in life.

May she pray for us now and at the hour of our death. Amen.

Also available from
Messenger Publications

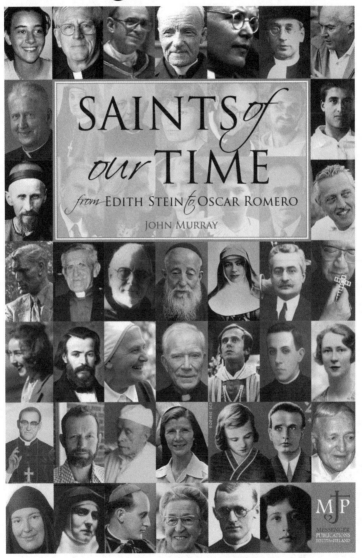

SAINTS *of our* TIME
from EDITH STEIN *to* OSCAR ROMERO
JOHN MURRAY